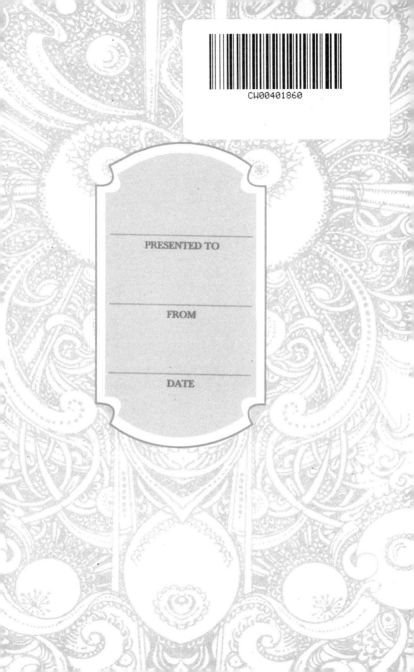

PRESENTED TO

FROM

DATE

Inspiring Thoughts

Price : ₹ 95/- (Rs. Ninety Five)

Edition : 2011
© Rajpal & Sons
ISBN : 978-81-7028-884-8
INSPIRING THOUGHTS OF RABINDRANATH TAGORE
compiled by Meera Johri
Printed at Deepika Enterprises., Delhi

RAJPAL & SONS, Kashmere Gate, Delhi-110006
website : www.rajpalpublishing.com
e-mail : sales@rajpalpublishing.com

Inspiring
Thoughts

RABINDRANATH TAGORE

Concept & Compilation
Meera Johri

rajpal

*W*here the mind is without fear
and the head is held high
Where knowledge is free
Where the world has not been broken up
into fragments by narrow domestic walls
Where words come out from the depth of truth
Where tireless striving
stretches its arms towards perfection
Where the clear stream of
reason has not lost its way
into the dreary desert sand of dead habit
Where the mind is led forward by thee
into ever-widening thought and action
Into that heaven of freedom,
my father,
let my country awake

We live in this world when we
love it

*M*an's abiding happiness is
not in getting anything
but in giving himself up
to what is greater than himself
to ideas which are
larger than his
individual self
The idea of his country
of humanity
of God

*D*o not say
It is morning
and
dismiss it with a name of yesterday
See it for the first time as
a new-born child that has no name

*L*et your life
lightly dance on the edges of Time
like dew on the tip of a leaf

*E*verything comes to us
that belongs to us
if we create the capacity
to receive it

*W*ith begging and scrambling
we find very little
But with being true to ourselves
we find a great deal more

$\mathcal{P}$rovidence expects that
we should make this world our own
and not live in it as though
it were a rented tenament
We can only make it
our own through some service
and that service is to lend it
love and beauty from our soul

I slept and dreamt that life was joy
I awoke and saw that life was service
I acted and behold service was joy

The meaning of our self is
not to be found in its separateness
from God and others
but in the ceaseless realisation
of yoga
of union

The same stream of life that
runs through my veins
night and day
runs through the world and
dances in rhythmic measures

$\mathcal{W}$e gain freedom when
we have paid the full price
for our right to live

Asks the Possible of the Impossible
'Where is your dwelling-place?'
'In the dreams of the Impotent'
comes the answer

$\mathcal{B}$eauty is truth's smile
when she beholds her own face
in a perfect mirror

*I*n love all the contradiction of existence
merge themselves and are lost
Only in love are
unity and duality not at variance
Love must be one and
two at the same time
Bondage and liberation
are not antagonistic in love
for love is most free and
at the same time most bound

*N*ot hammer strokes
but
dance of the water
sings the pebbles into perfection

I have spent my days
stringing and unstringing my instrument
while the song I came to sing
remains unsung

The butterfly counts not months
but moments
and has time enough

The emancipation
of our physical nature is
in attaining health
of our social being
in attaining goodness
and of our self
in attaining love

The potentiality of perfection
outweighs
actual contradictions

The fundamental desire of life
is the desire to exist

The most important lesson
that man can learn from his life is
not that there is pain in this world
but that it depends upon him
to turn it into good account
that it is possible for him to
transmute it into joy

The water in a vessel is sparkling
the water in the sea is dark
The small truth has words which are clear
the great truth has great silence

*W*hatever we treasure for ourselves
separates us from others
Our possessions are our limitations

Don't limit a child to your own learning
for he was born in another time

Death belongs to life
as birth does
The walk
is in the
raising of the foot
as in the
laying of it down

*F*acts are many
but the truth is one

To understand anything
is to find in it
something
which is our own and
it is the discovery of ourselves outside us
which makes us glad
This relation of understanding is partial
but the relation of love is complete

The mountain remains unmoved at seeming defeat by the mist

The tragedy of human life
consists in our vain attempts to
stretch the limits of things
which can never become unlimited
and to reach the infinite by
absurdly adding to the rungs
of the ladder of the finite

*T*hose who have everything
but thee my God
laugh at those who have
nothing but thyself.

The revealment of the infinite
in the finite
which is the motive of all creation
is not seen in its
perfection in the starry heavens
in the beauty of the flowers
It is in the soul of man

$\mathcal{I}$n its swelling pride
the bubble doubts
the truth of the sea
and laughs
and bursts into emptiness

The greed for fruit
misses the flower

To justify their own spilling of ink
they spell the day as night

My clouds sorrowing in the dark
forget that they themselves
have hidden the Sun

*I*am able to love my God
because He gives me freedom to
deny Him

*W*ealth is the burden of bigness
Welfare the fulness of being

To carry the burden of the instrument
count the cost of its material
and never to know that
it is for music
is the tragedy of deaf life

Open the door to that which must go
for the loss becomes unseemly
when obstructed

44

$\mathcal{T}$he tapestry of life's story
is woven with the threads of life's ties
ever joining and breaking

$\mathscr{I}$n my life's garden
my wealth has been
of the shadows and lights
that are never gathered and stored

$\mathcal{P}$rofit smiles on goodness
when the good is profitable

*M*an discovers his own wealth
when God comes to ask
gifts of him

The worm thinks it
strange and foolish
that man
does not eat his books

The sky remains infinitely vacant
for Earth there to build
its Heaven with dreams

*L*ife sends up
in blades of grass
its silent hymn of praise
to the unnamed Light

$\mathcal{L}$et me not grope in vain in the dark
but keep my mind still in the faith
that the day will break
and truth will appear
in its simplicity

Let me light my lamp
says the star
And never debate if
it will help to remove the darkness

*I*n the mountain
stillness surges up
to explore its own height
In the lake
movement stands still
to contemplate its own depth

*L*et me not pray to be
sheltered from dangers
but to be fearless
in facing them
Let me not beg
for the stilling of my pain
but for the heart to conquer it
Let me not look for
allies in life's battlefield
but to my own strength
Let me not cave in

Age considers
Youth ventures

While God waits
for His temple
to be built of love
men bring stones

The burden of self
is lightened
when I laugh at myself

Clouds come floating into my life
no longer to carry rain
or usher storm
but to add
colour to my sunset sky

$\mathscr{E}$very child comes with the message
that God is not yet
discouraged of man

These paper boats of mine
are meant to dance
on the ripples of hours
and not to reach
any destination

The sea of
danger
doubt and denial
around man's
little island of certainty
challenges him
to dare the unknown

*H*ills are the
Earth's gesture of despair
for the unreachable

To be outspoken is easy when
you do not wait to speak
the complete truth

We come nearest to the great when
we are great in humility

$\mathcal{T}$rees are Earth's endless efforts to speak to the listening Heavens

Taking shelter in the dead is
death itself
and only taking all the risk of life
to the fullest extent
is living

You can't cross the sea
merely by
standing and staring
at the water

*T*he touch of an infinite mystery
passes over the trivial and the familiar
making it break out
into ineffable music
The trees
the stars and
the blue hills
ache with a meaning
which can never
be uttered in words

The soil
in return for her service
keeps the tree tied to her
The sky asks nothing and
leaves it free

A mind all logic is like
a knife all blade
It makes the hand bleed
that uses it

Death is not extinguishing the light
It is putting out the lamp because
the dawn has come

*H*e who wants to do good
knocks at the gate
He who loves
finds the gate open

Want of love
is a degree of callousness
for love is the perfection
of consciousness
We do not love because
we do not comprehend or rather
we do not comprehend because
we do not love
For love is the ultimate meaning
of everything around us
It is not a mere sentiment
it is truth
it is the joy
that is at the root
of all creation

$\mathcal{I}$f you shut your door to all errors
truth will be shut out

If anger be the basis of
our political activities
the excitement tends to
become an end in itself
at the expense of
the object to be achieved
Such excitement is not
an exercise of strength
but a display of weakness

*I*n the night we stumble over things
and become acutely conscious
of their separateness
But the day reveals the unity
which embraces them

*I*n our desire for eternal life
we pray for an eternity of
our habit and comfort
forgetting that
immortality is in
repeatedly transcending
the definite forms of life
in order to pursue
the infinite truth of life

$\mathcal{O}$ur nature is obscured by
work done by
the compulsion of want or fear
The mother reveals herself in
the service of her children
so our true freedom is in action
which can only be attained
in the work of love

79

*L*ove does not claim possession
but gives freedom

*I*f life's journey be endless
where is its goal
The answer is
it is everywhere
We are in a palace which has no end
but which we have reached
By exploring it and
extending our relationship with it
we are ever making it
more and more our own

*L*eave out my name from the gift
if it be a burden
but keep my song

Let the dead
have the immortality of fame
but the living
the immortality of love

$\mathcal{L}$ife
like a child
laughs
shaking its rattle of death as it runs

*M*an goes into the noisy crowd
to drown his own
clamour of silence

The current of the world has its boundari
otherwise it could have no existence
But its purpose is not shown
in the boundaries which restrain it
but in its movement
which is toward perfection
The wonder is not that there should be
obstacles and sufferings in this world
but that there should be
law and order
beauty and joy
goodness and love

The fish in the water is silent
the animal on the earth is noisy
the bird in the air is singing
But man has in him
the silence of the sea
the noise of the earth and
the music of the air

$\mathcal{T}$ime is a wealth of change
but the clock in its parody
makes it mere change
and no wealth

From the solemn gloom of the temple
children run out to sit in the dust
God watches them play and
forgets the priest

$\mathcal{B}$irth is from the mystery of night
into the greater mystery of day

$\mathcal{T}$he tree is of today
the flower is old
it brings with it the message
of the immemorial seed

God's world
is ever renewed by death
A Titan's
ever crushed by its own existence

*B*eauty knows to say
enough
Barbarism clamours for still more

The picture
a memory of light
treasured by the shadow

The reed waits for his master's breath
the Master goes seeking for his reed

*G*od in His temple of stars
waits for man
to bring him his lamp

Child thou bringest to my heart
the babble of the wind and the water
the flower's speechless secrets
the cloud's dreams
the mute gaze of wonder
of the morning sky

$\mathcal{L}$et the evening forgive
the mistake of the day
and thus win peace for herself

The grass survives the hill
through its resurrections
from countless deaths

An unknown flower
in a strange land
speaks to the poet
Are we not of the same soil
my lover

*T*o the blind pen
the hand that writes is unreal
it's writing unmeaning

*W*hen I stand before thee
at the day's end
thou shalt see my scars and
know that I had
my wounds and
also my healing

*M*y last salutations are to them
who knew me imperfect
and loved me

When death comes and whispers to me
the days are ended
let me say to him
I have lived in love
and not in mere time
He will ask
will thy songs remain
I shall say I know not
but this I know
that often when I sang
I found my eternity